Masters of Music
THE WORLD'S GREATEST COMPOSERS

The Life and Times of

Richard Wagner

Mitchell Lane
PUBLISHERS

P.O. Box 196
Hockessin, Delaware 19707

Masters of Music
THE WORLD'S GREATEST COMPOSERS

Titles in the Series

The Life and Times of...

Visit us on the web: www.mitchelllane.com
Comments? email us: mitchelllane@mitchelllane.com

Masters of Music
THE WORLD'S GREATEST COMPOSERS

The Life and Times of
Richard Wagner

by Jim Whiting

Printing   1   2   3   4   5   6   7   8
    Library of Congress Cataloging-in-Publication Data
Whiting, Jim, 1943-
    The life and times of Richard Wagner / by Jim Whiting.
        p. cm. — (Masters of music)
    Includes bibliographical references (p.   ) and index.
    ISBN 1-58415-278-8 (library bound)
    1. Wagner, Richard, 1813-1883—Juvenile literature. 2. Composers—Germany—Biography—Juvenile literature. I. Title. II. Series: Masters of music (Mitchell Lane Publishers)
ML3930.W2W62 2004
782.1'092—dc22
[B]   2004002059

ABOUT THE AUTHOR: Jim Whiting has been a journalist, writer, editor, and photographer for more than 20 years. In addition to a lengthy stint as publisher of *Northwest Runner* magazine, Mr. Whiting has contributed articles to the *Seattle Times, Conde Nast Traveler, Newsday,* and *Saturday Evening Post.* He has edited more than 100 Mitchell Lane titles in the Real-Life Reader Biography series and Unlocking the Secrets of Science. A great lover of classical music, he has written many books for young adults, including *The Life and Times of Irving Berlin* and *The Life and Times of Frédéric Chopin* (Mitchell Lane). He lives in Washington state with his wife and two teenage sons.

PUBLISHER'S NOTE: This story is based on the author's extensive research, which he believes to be accurate. Documentation of such research is contained on page 47.

The internet sites referenced herein were active as of the publication date. Due to the fleeting nature of some web sites, we cannot guarantee they will all be active when you are reading this book.

Contents

The Life and Times of

Richard Wagner

by Jim Whiting

* For Your Information

Richard Wagner as he appeared at the time of his greatest success. His most famous work, The Ring of the Nibelung, *bears many resemblances to* The Lord of the Rings.

CHAPTER

I

Two Rings

I n the early 2000s, millions of people spent more than a
billion dollars to see an object about the size of a postage
stamp. This object was a golden ring. It appeared in three
movies, each of which is nearly three hours long: *The Fellowship of
the Ring, The Two Towers,* and *The Return of the King.* Taken together,
the three films are known as *The Lord of the Rings.*

As anyone familiar with the story knows, it is certainly no
ordinary ring. Forged by elves, it gives almost unimaginable power
to whoever has it. Unfortunately, not even good people can be
trusted to use this power wisely. Whoever has the ring is likely to
use it for evil purposes. The only solution to the problem is for a
hobbit named Frodo Baggins to take it into the very heart of the
empire of Mordor and destroy it by hurling it into Mount Doom.

This wasn't the first time that audiences flocked to see a story
about a ring with extraordinary powers. More than a century earlier,
people traveled vast distances to a small town in Germany for the
premiere of *Der Ring des Nibelungen (The Ring of the Nibelung).* Also
known as the Ring Cycle, it is the longest opera that has ever been
written. Like *The Lord of the Rings,* it consists of several shorter
parts. Because of the tremendous physical demands that it places

on its singers and the members of the orchestra, the Ring Cycle normally is presented over a period of between five and seven days.

The Ring Cycle opens with *Das Rheingold (The Rhinegold),* which is nearly three hours long. *Die Walküre (The Valkyrie)* and *Siegfried,* the second and third parts, are each about five hours in length. *Gotterdämmerung (The Twilight of the Gods),* which brings the opera to a close, lasts for about six hours. It is so long that it is sometimes performed with a dinner break. Yet hardly anyone ever gets restless while sitting through these long performances. The music is among the greatest that has ever been written, and the events on stage are so gripping that the time seems to go by quickly. Even today, productions of the Ring Cycle are normally sold out well over a year before the actual performances take place.

Left: This is a Valkyrie. Valkyries were mythological beings who picked up slain warriors and bore them to Valhalla, the home of the gods.

Right: Wotan, the chief god of German mythology, as he appears in a scene from the opera Siegfried.

Each of these two *Rings* has many different kinds of characters. *The Lord of the Rings* includes humans and hobbits, orcs and elves, Gimli and Gollum, wizards, and woods that come to life. *The Ring of the Nibelung* includes humans and half-humans, dwarfs and dragons, gods and giants, and mermaid-like creatures called the Rhinemaidens because they live in the Rhine River, Germany's most important river.

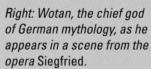

Left: A scene from Parsifal, *Wagner's final opera. It is about the search for the Holy Grail.*

Right: A scene near the end of Gotterdämmerung, *the final opera of the Ring Cycle. The hero Siegfried has just been killed.*

There are a number of other similarities. The rings themselves make whoever wears them invisible. A dragon guards a vast hoard of gold. A female gives up her immortality to marry a mortal man. Jealousy, betrayal, and murder frequently occur.

In both stories, a son is given a shattered sword that once belonged to his father. He then reforges it and uses it in battle.

It is interesting that the men who created the *Ring*'s both lost their fathers while they were still very young. Both were also very interested in the myths and sagas recorded in the Middle Ages and used that material extensively. Both men were almost revered by the time of their deaths. Otherwise, they were very different.

J.R.R. Tolkien, who wrote the books on which the movies are based, was a university professor. While he was aware of his fame, he never took advantage of it. He lived simply and quietly.

Richard Wagner (pronounced REEK-art VAHG-ner), the creator of *The Ring of the Nibelung,* had a huge ego. He makes most modern rock stars seem humble in comparison.

"I am not made like other people," he once said. "I must have brilliance and beauty and light. The world owes me what I need."[1]

He never hesitated to ask for what he needed. Once he requested money from a young nobleman he barely knew. To sweeten the deal, Wagner added what he thought would be a sure-fire "bonus." The young man would also provide him with free room and board for three months for the privilege of being close to him. The answer was no. Richard was astonished. He couldn't believe that anyone could turn him down.

Angrily the great man wrote back, "It probably will not happen again that a man like me will apply to you."[2]

Like many rock stars, he believed in living large. He spent lots of money—sometimes his own, more often what he borrowed or was given him—to furnish a lavish lifestyle.

His personality was so powerful that an estimated 10,000 books and articles were printed about him while he was still alive. Half a century after he died, one of the world's most evil men used his music to advance the cause of tyranny and oppression.

What is especially surprising is that in musical terms Wagner was a late bloomer. Unlike child prodigies such as Wolfgang Amadeus Mozart, Wagner was barely noticed until he was well into his thirties. But then he made up for lost time. Almost any short list of the world's greatest composers includes the name of Richard Wagner. ◆

A WRITER OF SHORTER STORIES

Hans Christian Andersen was born on April 2, 1805, in the city of Odense, Denmark. His father was a poor shoemaker and his mother was a washerwoman, so the boy grew up in poverty. Though he received little formal education, his father instilled in him a love of reading and often took him to the theater. Hans was sensitive and shy, and he often suffered real and imaginary illnesses.

When Hans was 11, his father died and Hans had to go to work. Three years later he ran away to Copenhagen, Denmark's capital and largest city. He had a beautiful soprano voice and tried to start a career in the theater. His voice soon changed and he had to give up that plan. Eventually some people befriended him and had him admitted to school. He had a difficult time because by then he was much older than the other pupils. His appearance—a long nose and eyes set very close together—attracted a great deal of teasing.

He entered the University of Copenhagen in 1828, and his play *Love in Saint Nicholas Church Tower* was produced in 1829. In 1831 he began traveling extensively in Europe. He published his first novel, *The Improvisatore,* in 1835.

Starting the same year and continuing for nearly four decades, he published *Fairy Tales and Stories,* for which he is most famous. Many of these stories are about characters who finally find happiness after long periods of suffering. They include "The Little Mermaid" (which later became a Disney movie), "The Ugly Duckling," "The Emperor's New Clothes," "The Steadfast Tin Soldier," "The Red Shoes," "The Princess and the Pea," and "The Snow Queen."

His final work was published in 1872. He died on August 4, 1875. His legacy lives on in the Hans Christian Andersen Medals, which are awarded every two years to one children's book author and one illustrator in honor of his or her entire body of work.

This is a picture of Johanna Wagner, the composer's mother. Richard was the last of her nine children with Carl Friedrich Wagner, who died a few months after Richard's birth. Within a year Johanna married Ludwig Geyer, a longtime family friend, who became very close to Richard. Unfortunately, Geyer died a few years later. Johanna lived until 1848.

Two Fathers

Wilhelm Richard Wagner was born on May 22, 1813, in Leipzig, Germany. His father was Carl Friedrich Wagner and his mother was Johanna Wagner. Richard was the youngest of the couple's nine children.

Other than the fact that Carl Friedrich Wagner was a police official, very little is known about Richard's father. He died before young Richard was even one year old, leaving his family with little money. He also left behind a mystery, because he might not have actually been Richard's father.

For some reason, a few weeks after Richard was born, Johanna made a trip of more than 100 miles to visit a family friend named Ludwig Geyer, a prominent actor and portrait painter. During that era, it was almost unheard of for a woman to make such a long, difficult trip over primitive roads by herself. In addition, the war against the French emperor Napoléon was being waged over much of German soil. It wasn't uncommon for civilians to be caught in the middle of the fighting, so Johanna was in a great deal of physical danger. Therefore she must have had a very powerful reason to make the trip. No one knows for certain what that reason was. Johanna never explained it. Some people believe the reason was that Geyer was actually Richard's father.

What is certain is Carl Friedrich died late in 1813, and Johanna married Geyer less than a year later. She and her new husband moved to Dresden, Germany. Soon afterward they had a daughter, Cäcilie. She would become Richard's favorite sibling.

It is also certain that young Richard adopted the name of his new stepfather and became known as Richard Geyer. The boy was close to Geyer, who took an immediate liking to him and nick-named him "The Cossack" because of his wild temperament. Geyer often commented that someday Richard would do great things. But he had no idea that it would be in music. In fact, no one had any idea that Richard had musical ability. Though Johanna made sure that most of her other children had music lessons, Richard wasn't one of them.

Not surprisingly, Richard's early interests were on the stage. When he was two, he appeared in a play as an angel, complete with tiny wings on his back. Two years later he had a one-line speaking part in *William Tell,* a popular play of the era. Shortly afterward, he attended his first opera.

A scene from the popular play William Tell. William Tell became a national hero in Switzerland when he killed an unpopular foreign ruler and encouraged the Swiss to seek their freedom. In a famous scene, he shoots an apple off his son's head with an arrow.

Richard was a small, thin boy who was often ill. There were times when his mother was afraid he would die. Her fears were not far-fetched. Childhood mortality was common then, and two of her other children had already died.

Geyer wanted to be sure that his son received a good education, so when Richard was seven, he sent him away to school in the nearby village of Possendorf. Richard was quickly summoned back home. Geyer had contracted tuberculosis, a common disease at that time. He died in September 1821. Richard's older siblings left home, many of them headed for careers as singers or actors. His older sister Rosalie became the family breadwinner.

For a while Richard lived with his uncle, Karl Friedrich. While he was there, he became interested in tightrope walking and acrobatics. Even when he was 60, he could amaze his friends by standing on his head.

When his uncle married, Richard moved back with his mother in Dresden. She was making extra money by renting out some of their rooms. Richard returned to school there in 1822. He received good marks for his conduct in class. He didn't do as well in many of his subjects, though he did become interested in Greek mythology. It was often hard for him to concentrate on school because he was still around actors and musicians. He began creating dramas in his own little puppet theater.

He still didn't show any aptitude for music, even after attending an opera called *Der Freischütz* by Carl Maria von Weber. The opera had a great effect on him, and the famous composer regularly walked by his house and occasionally stopped to chat. According to author Robert Gutman, "When von Weber, on meeting the nine-year-old Richard, politely asked him whether he wanted to be a musician, Frau Johanna informed the great man that, though the lad was mad about *Der Freischütz,* she had noticed no indication of musical talent."[1]

Soon afterward Richard started taking piano lessons. They didn't last long because he hated to practice.

In 1827, he and a friend decided to walk to Prague, a city in the modern-day Czech Republic. It was a journey of about 100 miles. At one point the boys found that they were flat broke. Richard stopped the first carriage that came along and begged for money. It was the beginning of a habit that would last for much of his life.

Later that year he moved back to Leipzig. *Wagner* soon replaced *Geyer* as Richard's last name. One reason might have been that Richard was becoming anti-Semitic and believed (falsely) that his stepfather was part Jewish. Another might have been that his uncle Adolf Wagner was famous in the city. With the same last name, his nephew could share in the older man's prestige. It also helped that hardly anyone in Leipzig knew Richard. That made it easier to establish his new identity.

More important for his development as a composer, Richard frequently heard the music of Ludwig van Beethoven and Mozart. These experiences had a profound effect on him. Music began to replace the theater as his main artistic interest. He dropped out of school to have more time to write music. He took violin lessons from a man named Robert Sipp. Richard wasn't very good. When Wagner became famous many years later, Sipp recalled that the young man had been his very worst pupil.

In 1830, a revolution in France resulted in the overthrow of King Charles X; he was replaced by King Louis-Philippe, who was considered more democratic. The success of the revolution led to revolts in other parts of Europe, and Richard took part in one that occurred in Leipzig. "The historical world began for me from this day; and naturally I was wholeheartedly for the revolution," he said.[2]

A revolution in 1830 made Louis-Philippe the king of France. But within a few years, he disappointed many people. This 1836 engraving compares Louis Philippe (on the left) very unfavorably with U.S. President Andrew Jackson (on the right).

Many university students became involved, and though Richard wasn't officially enrolled in college, he enjoyed hanging out with the students even after their revolutionary zeal began to wane. He often drank and gambled with them, and even joined a dueling society. Still slender and somewhat frail, he probably would have been seriously injured if he had had to fight. He also worked at a series of odd jobs and continued to write music. Late that year the B-flat Major Overture became his first composition to be performed in public. Hardly anyone was impressed. Some people even laughed. Red-faced with embarrassment, Richard snuck out the stage door.

Despite his earlier enthusiasm for Beethoven, Richard often seemed as if he were drifting with no purpose in life. He kept borrowing money and going further into debt. One day he even took his mother's money. He lost nearly all of it before his luck changed. He not only won it all back, but also won enough extra to pay off most of his debts.

He cared enough about his mother to realize that he had come very close to causing a lot of pain and embarrassment to her. Partly at her suggestion, in 1831 he began studying music with the cantor of a prominent local church, a man named Theodor Weinlig.

Weinlig taught him the importance of discipline. Soon Richard published his first work, the Sonata in B-flat Major. He dedicated it to Weinlig, who never charged him money for all the help he had given him. Those few months with Weinlig gave Richard the only formal musical training he ever had.

During this time, he also wrote his Symphony in C. Although symphonies were one of the most important musical forms of the late 18th and early 19th centuries—Beethoven and Franz Schubert each wrote 9, Mozart wrote 41, and Franz Joseph Haydn wrote 104—this was the only one that Wagner would ever write.

Wagner had already decided that opera was the field in which he wanted to specialize. He had also decided on one important difference between himself and other composers. He would write his own librettos—the words to the opera. In nearly every other case, operatic composers let someone else do the libretto. Wagner started working on *Die Hochzeit* (The Wedding), his first opera, during a visit to Prague in 1832, though he never completed it.

He was now nearly 20, an age when many composers had already written a great deal of music, especially in the case of such youthful geniuses as Mozart and Schubert. Yet Richard Wagner would spend nearly an entire decade experiencing almost no success, a great deal of instability, the likelihood of being arrested —and on several occasions, the possibility of suffering an early death.◆

FINDING TROY

Like Wagner, Heinrich Schliemann was fascinated by the myths of ancient Greece. Born in 1822 in Germany, Schliemann first read about the legendary war between the Trojans and Greeks when he was seven. He was enthralled by stories such as that of the Trojan horse. After 10 years of fighting, the Greek army hadn't been able to penetrate the walls of Troy. They pretended to sail away, leaving behind a large wooden horse, which was said to be a gift from the gods. The Trojans pulled it inside. That night, when everyone was asleep, a few Greeks who had hidden inside the horse crept out and opened the gates of the city. The rest of the Greek army had sailed back during the night. Thousands of warriors poured into the city and captured it.

Though Schliemann had to begin working when he was only 14, he proved to be a good businessman and became wealthy by the time he was still in his 20s. But his money didn't bring happiness. When one of his cousins died, he began to wonder about the purpose of his life.

At that time, most people believed that the Trojan War was just a legend. Schliemann believed otherwise. He felt sure that Troy had actually existed. He wanted to find it. He went to Greece in 1868 and asked a friend to find him a young woman to marry. Schliemann and his bride, Sophie, went to Turkey and started digging at the site of what he believed was the ancient city. After several years, they found a hoard of golden objects. Schliemann was convinced that he had found Troy.

He returned to Greece and began excavating a site called Mycenae, which had been the home of King Agamemnon, the leader of the Greek army that invaded Troy. Schliemann was also successful there.

He spent the rest of his life in Greece, where he died in 1890.

This is probably the most famous picture of Richard Wagner. By this time, he had become internationally famous. The personal and financial struggles of his earlier years were only a memory.

Failures and First Successes

Because Germany consisted of dozens of large and small kingdoms during most of Richard's lifetime, there were numerous musical opportunities for composers. Many cities and towns had their own theaters and musical groups.

Richard joined his older brother Albert in 1833 in the city of Würzburg, where Richard became the chorus master in the local theater. He had another reason for leaving Leipzig. He was at an age where he probably would have been drafted into the army.

When he was in Würzburg, he worked on another opera, which he called *Die Feen (The Fairies)*. Though he quickly completed it, it was never performed while he was alive. The following year he moved to Magdeburg, where he was appointed as the theater's music director. There he composed his second opera, *Das Liebesverbot (The Ban on Love)*. Its premiere was a disaster. There was no advertising, none of the singers knew their parts, and the audience had no idea what was going on. Word quickly got out and only three people bought tickets for the scheduled second performance a few days later. Just before the curtain went up, the main singer and her husband got into a violent argument. The other cast members took sides and began throwing punches at one another. The performance was canceled.

About the same time, Wagner met an actress named Minna Planer, who was four years older than Richard. Since life in the theater could be very uncertain financially, Minna's main goal was to find someone with a secure, stable career to marry. The young Richard didn't seem to fit that category, but he pursued her, even after they continued to have violent arguments. Finally, they were married in November 1836. Soon afterward she left town with a man who had more money than Richard, but the man eventually abandoned her. She wrote to Richard to beg his forgiveness. They were reunited in the city of Riga in modern-day Latvia, where Richard had managed to get a job as music director. They settled there. Minna kept house while Richard worked with his small orchestra and composed his first large opera, *Rienzi*.

Minna Wagner, Richard's first wife. She supported him through his early struggles and remained faithful for many years.

It didn't take Richard long to realize that Riga was not the right place to present an ambitious opera such as *Rienzi*. He and Minna decided it was time to expand their horizons. They set their sights on Paris, which at that time had Europe's finest opera house. Even better from Richard's point of view, it paid large royalties. Its appeal was greater still because his sister Cäcilie was living there with her husband.

There was only one problem with this plan: The Wagners had accumulated a lot of debt while living in Riga. Their creditors were demanding payment and even threatening to throw Richard into prison. In order to leave Riga, they had to sneak out. Their problem was more complicated because Richard—a dog lover during his entire life—insisted on taking Robber, their huge Newfoundland, with them.

First they had to sprint across a border heavily patrolled by armed horsemen who had orders to shoot to kill. Fortunately, Robber didn't bark, or they would have been discovered. On the way to the seaport where they would board a ship, their carriage overturned. Minna was pinned underneath and suffered serious internal injuries. Richard was flung onto a pile of horse manure.

Their problems continued even after their ship departed. Their plan was to sail to London, England, then cross the English Channel to Paris. The voyage to London took nearly a month. Most of the time they were battling strong headwinds and violent storms. At one point, Minna became so frightened that she asked to be tied to her husband. That way they would drown together. The terrifying trip did have one positive effect. It provided Richard with the idea for his next opera, *Der fliegende Holländer (The Flying Dutchman)*.

After spending a week in London, Richard, Minna, and Robber left for France. It was not a successful venture. Hardly anyone paid any attention to him, though he worked very hard. In addition to composing music, he also wrote articles for magazines and reviewed concerts. But none of these activities paid very well. He was further handicapped because he didn't play any instruments, so he couldn't make money by performing in public. As a result, the Wagners experienced serious financial problems and lived in poverty. Richard may even have been thrown in jail for a brief time.

Born in 1791, Giacomo Meyerbeer was the most famous opera composer during the time that the Wagners were living in Paris. He died in 1864.

Richard's ego was already large. He believed that he deserved better treatment. He became jealous of almost anyone who was successful. One such man was the pianist and composer Franz Liszt. Though Liszt was only two years older than Richard, he had already achieved a great deal of fame for his virtuoso piano playing. Richard was even more resentful toward Giacomo Meyerbeer, the most successful composer of operas at that time. Meyerbeer freely offered assistance and advice to Richard. It didn't matter. Richard soon turned against Meyerbeer, at least partly because he was Jewish. It wasn't the last time that Richard would bite the hand that fed him.

He did manage to complete *Rienzi* and *The Flying Dutchman* while he was living in Paris. But the experience left him with life-long bitterness against both the city and "the Jews," whom he blamed for many of his misfortunes.

In 1842, *Rienzi* was accepted for performance in Dresden—partly because of Meyerbeer's recommendation. Not long afterward, an opera company in Berlin offered to produce *The Flying Dutchman*. It seemed apparent to Richard that his future was back in his native country. Richard and Minna returned to Dresden.

Even though it was nearly six hours long, *Rienzi* proved to be a huge hit. Its success led directly to Richard's appointment as the city's royal kapellmeister. He would be in charge of all the music in the city. For his long-suffering wife, it seemed almost too good to be true.

It was. Even though *The Flying Dutchman* was performed the following year, Richard felt that people didn't appreciate him enough. Perhaps they just weren't used to his style—*The Flying Dutchman* was very different from other operas of that era. *Tännhauser,* which followed two years later, was even more so. Though Wagner was discouraged, it didn't keep him from composing. He began working on *Lohengrin,* which contains one of the most famous musical compositions of all time. The "Bridal Chorus," or "Here Comes the Bride," as it is more commonly known, is played at the beginning of nearly every American wedding.

Another source of conflict was an elaborate plan Wagner submitted to restructure the theater. His main argument was that his operas would sound better, but he also included provisions that would bring more job security to everyone from lead singers to janitors. His plan was rejected.

By then it was 1848. Once again, revolutions were breaking out all over Europe. Revolution was also in Wagner's head. He conceived the bare outline of a musical drama unlike anything the world had known since the days of ancient Greece. He called it a "Sketch for the Nibelung Myth as Basis for a Drama." Soon he began writing the libretto for the opera. It would take 28 years to complete the entire project.

In the meantime, there was some doubt as to whether Wagner himself would complete one more year.

The Orient Express is probably the world's best-known train. This is how it appeared in the 1930s during the peak of its fame.

This old-fashioned steam engine is similar to the ones that were used during the final years of the 19th century, when the Orient Express was beginning its service.

A FAMOUS TRAIN

During Wagner's lifetime, trains became one of the most important technological advances in improving travel. One of the world's most famous trains is the Orient Express. In its heyday—between World War I and World War II—it conjured up images of romance, intrigue, and even murder. Agatha Christie wrote a mystery novel entitled *Murder on the Orient Express* in 1934. It became a popular 1974 film, with more than a dozen big-name stars such as Sean Connery, Albert Finney, and Lauren Bacall. In 2001, CBS used the book as the basis for a made-for-television movie.

The train's origins go back to 1876, when a Belgian named Georges Nagelmackers founded La Compagnie Internationale des Wagons-Lits to provide luxurious railroad sleeping and dining cars. His efforts were similar to what George Pullman was doing in the United States at the same time.

In 1883, Nagelmackers set the Express d'Orient in motion. It ran twice a week from Paris through Strasbourg, France; Munich, Germany; Vienna, Austria; Budapest, Hungary; and Bucharest and Giurgiu, Romania. At that point, passengers would cross the Danube River on a ferry to Ruse, Bulgaria. There they would board trains for a seven-hour trip to Varna, a seaport on the Black Sea. A fourteen-hour voyage across the sea to Istanbul, Turkey, completed the trip.

Six years later the railway line was completed all the way to Istanbul. In 1891, the train's name was changed to Orient Express. After World War I, a second, more southernly route—the Simplon Orient Express—ran from Paris to Istanbul. Soon the two trains were carrying thousands of passengers every week.

With the availability of passenger airplanes and improved roads after World War II, the Orient Express had a hard time competing. In 1977, the overland service to Istanbul was ended. In the 1980s, the Orient Express began providing overnight service only between Paris and Budapest and between Paris and Vienna.

Today the tradition also lives on in the Venice Simplon Orient Express, which runs from London and Paris to Venice, and the American Orient Express, which operates in North America. They both include restored railroad cars that carry travelers to various destinations in luxury and splendor.

Franz Liszt is perhaps the world's greatest pianist. During his eight years of concert tours that began in 1839, audiences displayed the same frenzied adulation that modern rock stars enjoy.

Continuing Struggles

I n the spring of 1849, it was Dresden's turn to join the wave of popular revolutions. After a period of instability, troops poured into the city to put down the uprising. Some of the rebels were given summary executions—shot on the spot without a trial. Because Richard had actively supported the revolt, orders were issued for his arrest. If he had been caught, he too might have been executed.

Wagner fled to nearby Weimar, where Franz Liszt had recently become the kapellmeister after retiring from his spectacular concert career. Liszt was aware of Richard's growing reputation and was arranging a production of *Tännhauser*. One of the most generous men in musical history, Liszt sheltered the fugitive for a brief time. Then he gave Richard enough money to go to Zurich, Switzerland, where he would be safer. Again Wagner had to sneak away from a bad situation.

Once he was safe from arrest, Richard wrote "Jewishness in Music," which illustrated his anti-Semitic views. He continued to blame the Jews for his problems.

More positively, he also wrote several long essays that spelled out his artistic vision in detail. His recent works such as *Tännhauser* and *Lohengrin* reflected that vision. He was more interested in writing what he called "music dramas" than in traditional operas.

He also wanted to demonstrate his belief about the superiority of the German people. His early interest in Greek mythology gave way to the great medieval legends surrounding German heroes, and he resumed working on the libretto of the *Ring of the Nibelung.* Interestingly, he had started with the end of the opera and worked his way back to its starting point. He finished the libretto in 1852. It was already clear that this would be no ordinary opera. He included elaborate stage directions, many of which exceeded the capacity of existing technology. Another difference was that there would be no arias. Customary in most other operas, arias are solos that show off the singers' abilities. When the last notes are completed, there is an extended pause while the audience applauds. Richard didn't want any such breaks in his unfolding drama.

With the libretto completed, he began the more difficult task of writing the music. He completed *Rhinegold* in 1854, *The Valkyrie* two years later, and began *Siegfried* soon afterward.

Then he put *Siegfried* aside to begin writing an opera based on the medieval legend of Tristan and Isolde. Theirs is the story of a love triangle, and it may have been inspired by events that were taking place in Wagner's own life. He was becoming more and more involved with a woman named Mathilde Wesendonck, whom he had met soon after arriving in Zurich. Mathilde's husband, Otto, was a wealthy businessman, and he helped to support Richard financially. Mathilde adored Richard. She supported him by encouraging him to continue composing.

Of course, the presence of another woman in Richard's life didn't make Minna happy. Their relationship got even worse when Richard set several of Mathilde's love poems to music, called the

Mathilde Wesendonck was one of Richard Wagner's greatest admirers. His wife was jealous of the attention he paid to Mathilde.

Wesendonck Lieder. According to one story, Minna bought a parrot and taught it to say, "Wagner is a bad husband."[1]

The situation came to a head late in 1857. Otto Wesendonck had provided a cottage for Richard and Minna on the grounds of his estate. Mathilde's visits to the composer became even more frequent. No one is sure how close they really were, but Minna read a letter from Mathilde to Richard and believed that he was cheating on her. She went home to Dresden.

Richard traveled to Venice, Italy, then back to Switzerland, where he finished *Tristan and Isolde.* During this period, he often wrote to Minna, asking her forgiveness. She relented, and then Otto Wesendonck gave him another large sum of money. Richard and Minna made one final visit to Paris, where his *Tännhauser* was booed off the stage. By this time, he had been granted an amnesty by German authorities, so he could finally return. But he didn't stay long.

In 1862, he traveled to Vienna, Austria—by himself. Minna had finally had enough. She left him, this time for good. They would never see each other again. After settling down in Vienna, Richard began borrowing huge sums of money. He felt sure that success was just around the corner.

It wasn't. Again he found himself deep in debt and having trouble paying it off. According to Austrian law, there were harsh penalties for late debt payments. Again he had to sneak away, and again he went to Switzerland. He thought of marrying a woman—any woman—with a lot of money. First he had to divorce Minna. Since she wasn't speaking to him, he asked one of his sisters to contact Minna and request a divorce. The sister refused.

Then he had an astonishing stroke of luck.

Richard Wagner performs for a select group of music lovers. While we can't be sure, it's very likely that the music he's playing is his own. Wagner had a huge ego and wanted people to listen to his music.

A FAMOUS EXPLORER

Explorer David Livingstone was born in 1813, the same year as Richard Wagner, in a village near Glasgow, Scotland. At the age of 10 he began working 14-hour shifts in a local cotton mill, then spent several hours attending school at night.

When he was 23, he entered medical school. Because of his Christian upbringing, he wanted to become a missionary in Africa after he finished. He landed in South Africa in 1841 and made his way northward into the heart of the continent. His main goals were to convert the inhabitants to Christianity, and to work to end the slave trade. In 1855, he discovered Victoria Falls, one of the world's most spectacular water-falls. He became a national hero when he returned to England in 1856 and wrote a best-selling book, *Missionary Travels*.

His second trip wasn't as successful. His wife became ill and died, and his efforts against the slave trade proved futile.

He went to Africa for a third and final time in 1865. The Royal Geo-graphic Society wanted him to find the source of the Nile River. Several years went by and there was no word from or about him. Late in 1869 the *New York Herald* dispatched Henry Stanley, one of its best reporters, to search for Livingstone. Stanley began his expedition in March 1871. Seven months later, he entered a village and an elderly man came up to him.

"Dr. Livingstone, I presume?" Stanley asked the man.

Stanley had brought badly needed food and medicine. Livingstone was ill with malaria. He recovered some of his strength, then set off on his own again. Soon he suffered a relapse. He was taken to a native village, where he died in May 1873. Following the local custom, his heart was buried under a nearby tree. The rest of his body was sent back to England and buried in Westminster Abbey on what was declared a national day of mourning.

Richard Wagner's second wife Cosima was the daughter of Franz Liszt. She and Wagner had three children together.

King Ludwig and Cosima

E arly in May 1864, Richard was approached by a man claiming to be the official representative of the king of Bavaria, one of the largest German kingdoms. Suspecting that the man was simply a bill collector using a creative way to approach him, Richard didn't pay any attention.

The man persisted. Eventually he convinced Richard that he was genuine.

The two men traveled to Munich, the capital of Bavaria. Richard met Ludwig II, the newly crowned 18-year-old king. Ludwig was an impressionable boy who had grown up with legends of knighthood and chivalry. The castle in which he was raised was covered with murals depicting the legend of Lohengrin, a heroic German knight. He saw a production of Richard's opera *Lohengrin* when he was 15, and decided that his destiny was to help out the opera's creator.

He paid Richard's debts and gave him a mansion in Munich. Richard showed his gratitude by immediately spending huge amounts of the king's money to decorate it. Several rooms were draped in satin and velvet. Expensive French perfumes were sprayed throughout the interior. Equally expensive rare flowers provided touches of color.

An elegant place to live was only the start. Richard told Ludwig that he needed much more. A new theater. A new music school where singers could learn the techniques they'd need to perform his operas. Richard assured Ludwig that he would gain a great deal of prestige by presenting his operas. Munich would become one of Europe's most important cultural centers.

Ludwig happily complied. "Now that the royal purple enfolds me," he told Richard, "I will use it to sweeten your life."[1]

To oversee all these changes, Richard believed that he had the perfect man: a conductor named Hans von Bülow. Von Bülow's professional qualifications weren't the only reason for Richard's interest. Several years earlier, the conductor had married Franz

Hans von Bülow was one of the most famous conductors of the 19th century. He often conducted Wagner's works.

Liszt's daughter Cosima. The honeymooning couple had visited Richard when he was still living with the Wesendoncks. In 1863, Richard visited the von Bülows in Berlin. He was desperately seeking feminine companionship and took Cosima for a carriage ride. While she already had two children with von Bülow, Cosima wasn't very happy in her marriage. Although Richard was 50 and Cosima was 26, theirs was apparently a case of love at first sight. She was also much taller than Richard, who stood barely five feet, six inches.

Early the following summer, Cosima and her two young daughters traveled to Munich, where they stayed with Richard. Von Bülow arrived a week later and quickly realized that all was not as it should be. He tried to make the best of a bad situation.

The following April, Cosima gave birth to a daughter, whose name Isolde suggested that Richard was the father, which in fact he was. But everyone felt that it was important to keep up appearances. Von Bülow was listed as the infant's father. Despite the pain he must have felt, von Bülow stayed in Munich to conduct the premiere of *Tristan and Isolde.*

King Ludwig II of Bavaria assumed the throne when he was just 18. He supported Richard Wagner at a crucial period in the composer's life.

The opera was a triumph, but it didn't take long for Richard to find himself in trouble once again. Several important people in King Ludwig's government hated him. Many Bavarians believed that the 52-year-old composer had too much influence over the young monarch. As usual, Richard contributed to his own problems. He publicly referred to the young Ludwig as "Mein Junge" (my boy). Bavaria was a conservative, very Catholic kingdom, and his relationship with Cosima also created a scandal. In December he was ordered to leave the kingdom. Once again he sought refuge in Switzerland. Ludwig still believed in him and continued to send him money. Richard settled on the shore of Lake Lucerne in a house that he called Triebschen.

Under the baton of von Bülow, his opera *Die Meistersinger von Nürnberg (The Mastersingers of Nuremberg)* premiered in Munich in June 1868. It was Richard's biggest triumph to date.

Things were still somewhat chaotic personally. For some reason, he decided to reissue "Jewishness in Music." Many audiences booed his music because of the essay. But in some parts of Germany, it struck a responsive chord—which would bear fruit several generations later with Adolf Hitler and the Holocaust.

Even though Richard and Cosima were mostly living apart to keep up appearances, she gave birth to their daughter Eva in 1867, and son Siegfried followed in June 1869.

Over Richard's objections, *The Rhinegold*—the first of the four Ring operas—was produced in Munich that same year, with *The Valkyrie* following in 1870. Though both operas were well received, Richard sulked. He didn't believe the opera house in Munich was large enough to do justice to his works.

Soon afterward, Cosima obtained a divorce from von Bülow. She and Richard were married in August 1870. Richard was a Protestant. He insisted that Cosima renounce her Catholic faith. She agreed. Her father was horrified. A lifelong Catholic, he had taken Holy Orders several years earlier. It would be several years before father and daughter would resume friendly relations.

On Christmas Day that year, Cosima awoke to find that her new husband had snuck a small orchestra into the house. The musicians played a piece he had composed specifically for her as a present. Called *Siegfried Idyll,* it is still popular today.

With his personal life in order for the first time in many years, the stage was set for the greatest triumph of Richard Wagner's life.

After putting it aside for more than a decade to work on other projects, he resumed composing *The Ring of the Nibelung.* It was almost as if he had never taken a break. He finished *Siegfried* in 1871, and *Twilight of the Gods* came to completion three years later.

Because of the number of characters, the plot is very complex. To help the audience understand what is happening, Richard employed what he called leitmotifs. Every character and every important prop has a distinctive musical signature. When that music is played, the audience would recognize who or what was onstage.

The next step was to actually stage *The Ring of the Nibelung.* Typically, Richard believed that no existing opera house was big enough or had the technical facilities he needed. He wanted to build a new structure specifically to stage the *Ring.* It would be the site of a festival devoted entirely to his works. It didn't take him long to find an ideal location.

Richard had visited the town of Bayreuth in 1836, and it held pleasant memories for him. He and Cosima went there in 1871. The townspeople were receptive to the idea of erecting Richard's proposed theater and holding the festival there. It had a good location, close to the center of Germany. All Richard needed was enough money to start construction.

Villa Wahnfried in Bayreuth, Germany, was Richard Wagner's home for the last decade of his life. He was buried there.

The Festspielhaus (theater) at Bayreuth. Wagner designed it especially so that his operas could be performed there.

In the meantime, Richard was enjoying the plight of Paris. The city had been quickly surrounded by the invading Germany army in the Franco-Prussian War, which would soon lead to the establishment of a united Germany. The Parisians were reduced to eating rats because no food could get through the German blockade. Remembering his unhappy experiences there, Richard publicly called for the city to be destroyed. Fortunately, hardly anyone paid attention.

By this time, he was famous enough that Wagner societies began springing up all across the newly united country to raise money. For a substantial donation, people would be guaranteed seats at the festival. But the plan didn't work out. The project fell behind schedule. Then Ludwig came through again. The young king advanced Wagner enough money to complete the project. The Wagners also built a home in Bayreuth, which they named Villa Wahnfried. Things were definitely looking up. Even Liszt was beginning to thaw.

The premiere of *The Ring of the Nibelung* in 1876 attracted world-wide interest. People came from all around the globe to attend. The response was almost entirely favorable.

Richard's reputation was finally cemented. His operas were being performed all over Europe. By this time the payment of royalties had become steady, so his financial worries were over.

Ill health barely slowed him down. It appears likely that all the stress he had gone through during his life finally caught up with him. He suffered a variety of illnesses and began making trips to Italy, hoping that the better climate there would improve his health.

The illnesses did slow him down, however. He continued to write books and essays on a wide variety of subjects. He also worked on *Parsifal,* which would be his final opera.

Parsifal premiered in Bayreuth in 1882. During its sixteenth and final performance, Richard left his seat and went to the stage to conduct the last act. Soon afterward, he and his family traveled to Venice. He would never again see his beloved Germany.

On February 13, 1883, Richard suffered a fatal heart attack. His body was taken back to Bayreuth. The entire town mourned its most famous citizen. His son Siegfried had to calm the dogs, who were howling for their master. Richard Wagner was laid to rest in the grounds of Villa Wahnfried.

His life had come to an end. The controversies that had swirled around him while he was alive would continue.

"Richard Wagner was a dreadful human being," says author Phil Goulding. "He was a liar, a cheat, a wife-stealer, a home-wrecker, and a betrayer of friends. He was anti-Semitic, anti-Catholic, and anti-French. He was immoral and dishonorable. No one in music had a bigger ego, and he properly belongs high on a list of the World's Most Unpleasant Men."

"He was also, of course, an incredible music genius. It is impossible to like Wagner, but almost equally impossible to deny his genius."[2]

A new production of the *Ring of the Nibelung* was presented in 1976 in Bayreuth. The opera was set during Richard's own times, rather than the traditional Viking-era staging in which characters wore costumes such as helmets with wings on them. Now they wore clothing that Richard would have been familiar with. On opening night, there was nearly a riot. Part of the audience loved it. Part hated it. Both sides screamed at each other. Fistfights broke out. The wife of Wolfgang Wagner, the composer's grandson and the manager of the Bayreuth Festival, was caught in a scuffle, and her dress was nearly torn apart. Another woman had part of her ear ripped off.

Wagner's music was also put to a much darker use. Six years after the composer died, the future Nazi German dictator Adolf Hitler was born. When Hitler was still a boy, he attended a production of Wagner's opera *Rienzi* and claimed that during the performance he had a vision of his future political career. "That was the hour it all began," Hitler said later in his life.[3] He also said, "Whoever wants to understand National Socialist [Nazi] Germany must know Wagner."[4]

Hitler shared many of Wagner's ideas, especially the composer's anti-Semitism and his belief in the superiority of the German people. He attended many performances of Wagner's operas and insisted that his followers do the same, even saying on one occasion, "On the day following the end of the Bayreuth Festival I'm gripped by a great sadness—as when one strips the Christmas tree of its ornaments."[5] He ordered Wagner's music to be played during Nazi party rallies. He became close friends with Winifred Wagner, the wife of the composer's son Siegfried, and often visited them at Villa Wahnfried. As the Russian, British, and American armies closed in around him at the end of World War II, he envisioned dying in a blaze of glory such as at the conclusion of *Twilight of the Gods.*

Before Hitler died, he was responsible for the atrocities of the Holocaust, including the deaths of six million Jews in concentration camps such as Auschwitz, Treblinka, and Dachau. After the Jewish state of Israel was established in 1948, most of its citizens made a close connection between Adolf Hitler and Richard Wagner. They regarded Wagner as a symbol of the Nazis. When an orchestra in Israel tried to play some of his music in 1981—thirty-six years after the war had ended—many people were still so upset that there was nearly a riot. It wasn't until the year 2000 that Wagner's music was finally played live in Israel. Even then, some people objected.

Others were more willing to let Wagner's music be performed. One Israeli musician said, "Wagner died 50 years before Hitler came to power. Moreover, he was a kind of private anti-Semite, refusing to sign any public declarations against the Jews. He actually worked with many Jews."[6]

The controversy seems likely to go on. Richard Wagner's life and music continue to inspire strong feelings.

THE MAD KING OF BAVARIA

King Ludwig II was born in 1845 in the German state of Bavaria. At that time, Germany consisted of many kingdoms. Bavaria was among the largest and most important of these. Ludwig, who was a shy boy with a vivid imagination, spent much of his time by himself. By the age of 12, he had already seen some of Richard Wagner's operas and was very impressed with them. In 1864, his father died and Ludwig became king. One of his first acts was to invite Wagner to move to Bavaria. Ludwig was very generous with his support for the composer, even after Wagner's huge demands made almost everyone else very angry with him. For many years the Bavarian capital city of Munich was a major location for opera in Europe.

Later in his reign, Ludwig began building elaborate castles that were idealized versions of those built during the Middle Ages. The most famous of those is Neuschwanstein, which means "new swan stone" in German. Swans were Ludwig's favorite animals.

Unfortunately, Ludwig's extravagant castle construction nearly exhausted the Bavarian treasury. In 1886, Ludwig was declared insane and was forced to give up his throne. Soon afterward, he and his personal physician were found drowned in a nearby lake. No one knows whether Ludwig committed suicide or was murdered.

Though Neuschwanstein was never completed during Ludwig's lifetime, its soaring towers became the model for the castle in the Walt Disney film *Sleeping Beauty*. It was also used for scenes in the movies *Chitty Chitty Bang Bang* and *Around the World in 80 Days*. Its picture appears in many advertisements for German tourism.

Today Neuschwanstein and Ludwig's other castles are some of Bavaria's main attractions, with more than 6,000 visitors daily. The buildings that almost bankrupted Bavaria have become one of its main sources of income.

Selected Works

Operas

Der Ring des Nibelungen (The Ring of the Nibelung)
—Das Rheingold (The Rhinegold)
—Die Walküre (The Valkyrie)
—Siegfried (Siegfried)
—Gotterdämmerung (Twilight of the Gods)
Rienzi
Der fliegende Holländer (The Flying Dutchman)

Tännhauser
Lohengrin
Tristan und Isolde
Die Meistersinger von Nürnberg (The Mastersingers of Nuremberg)
Parsifal

Orchestral Works

Siegfried Idyll
Symphony in C

Chronology

1813 Wilhelm Richard Wagner born on May 22; his father, Carl Friedrich Wagner, dies
1814 Mother, Johanna Wagner, marries Ludwig Geyer; Richard takes last name of Geyer
1820 Begins school in Possendorf
1821 Ludwig Geyer dies
1822 Begins school in Dresden
1828 Takes name of Richard Wagner
1831 Studies under Christian Theodor Weinlig
1834 Becomes musical director of theater company in Magdeburg
1836 Marries Minna Planer
1837 Becomes theater director in Riga, Latvia
1839 Flees Latvia
1842 Opera Rienzi premieres
1843 Becomes royal kapellmeister in Dresden
1848 Begins sketches for Ring of the Nibelung; becomes involved in political revolutions
1849 Tännhauser is performed with the assistance of Franz Liszt
1852 Completes Ring of the Nibelung as a drama
1857 Begins Tristan and Isolde
1859 Completes Tristan and Isolde
1862 Sees Minna for the final time
1864 Receives financial and moral support from King Ludwig II of Bavaria; begins affair with Cosima (Liszt) von Bülow
1865 Birth of daughter Isolde
1866 Moves to Lucerne, Switzerland; Minna dies
1867 Birth of daughter Eva
1869 Birth of son Siegfried
1870 Marries Cosima
1872 Moves to Bayreuth, Germany, and begins construction of theater Festspielhaus
1876 Premieres Ring of the Nibelung in Bayreuth
1877 Begins Parsifal
1882 Completes Parsifal, and it premieres in Bayreuth
1883 Dies in Venice, Italy, on February 13

Timeline in History

1811 Composer Franz Liszt is born.

1819 The U.S. ship *Savannah* becomes the first steamship to cross the Atlantic Ocean; the United States purchases Florida from Spain.

1825 Composer Ludwig van Beethoven's Ninth Symphony premieres.

1832 Louisa May Alcott, the future author of *Little Women*, is born.

1833 Alfred Nobel, who would invent dynamite and whose fortune is the source for Nobel Prizes awarded every year, is born.

1837 Queen Victoria begins her 63-year reign as queen of England.

1843 Charles Dickens writes *A Christmas Carol*.

1846 Belgian instrument maker Adolphe Sax patents his invention, the saxophone.

1850 Robert Louis Stevenson, who will write *Treasure Island*, is born.

1855 Scottish missionary and explorer David Livingstone discovers Victoria Falls in Africa.

1858 German auto engineer Rudolf Diesel is born.

1861 The U.S. Civil War begins.

1864 Ludwig II becomes king of Bavaria.

1865 President Abraham Lincoln is assassinated; U.S. Civil War ends.

1868 Wilkie Collins writes *The Moonstone*, one of the first detective novels.

1871 The German kingdom of Prussia wins the Franco-Prussian War, which results in the unification of Germany; reporter Henry Stanley finds Livingstone in Africa.

1874 Winston Churchill, the English leader during World War II, is born.

1876 Alexander Graham Bell patents the telephone.

1883 The Brooklyn Bridge in New York City opens to traffic.

1886 Franz Liszt dies.

1889 German dictator Adolf Hitler is born.

1930 Cosima Wagner dies.

Glossary

anti-Semitic (AN-tie-seh-MIH-tik)—prejudiced against Jews.

aria (AR-ee-ah)—an elaborate solo, usually sung as part of an opera.

cantor (KAN-ter)—director of music at a German Protestant church.

Cossack (KAH-sak)—skilled Russian cavalryman with a reputation for wildness.

kapellmeister (keh-PELL-my-ster)—the leader of an orchestra at the court of a nobleman.

libretto (lih-BREH-toe)—the words of a musical composition, such as an opera.

motif (moe-TEEF)—a recurring element or idea in a work of art.

movement—shorter compositions that form the sections of a longer work such as a symphony, concerto, or sonata.

opera (AH-p'rah)—a drama set to music, with all or most of the dialogue sung.

prodigy (PRAH-deh-jee)—an exceptionally gifted young person.

royalties—fees paid to an artist for each copy or performance of his or her work.

saga (SAH-guh)—a story about the heroic figures of ancient or medieval Iceland and Norway.

sonata (sew-NAH-tuh)—a composition for one or two instruments, typically with three or four contrasting movements.

soprano (seh-PRAH-noh)—the highest singing voice among the five levels of singers; the others in descending order are alto, tenor, baritone and bass.

symphony (SIM-foe-nee)—a large-scale musical composition for full orchestra, usually consisting of four movements.

virtuoso (vir-choo-OH-so)—an extremely skilled musician.

Chapter Notes

Chapter 1   Two Rings

1. Phil G. Goulding, *Classical Music: The 50 Greatest Composers and Their 1,000 Greatest Works* (New York: Ballantine Books, 1992), p. 152.

2. Harold Schonberg, *The Lives of the Great Composers* (New York: W. W. Norton, 1981), p. 274.

Chapter 2   Two Fathers

1. Robert W. Gutman, *Richard Wagner: The Man, His Mind, and His Music* (New York: Time Life Records, 1972), p. 13.

2. Derek Watson, *Richard Wagner: A Biography* (New York: Schirmer Books, 1979), p. 31.

Chapter 4   Continuing Struggles

1. William Berger, *Wagner Without Fear* (New York: Vintage Books, 1998), p. 29.

Chapter 5   King Ludwig and Cosima

1. Robert W. Gutman, *Richard Wagner: The Man, His Mind, and His Music* (New York: Time Life Records, 1972), p. 250.

2. Phil G. Goulding, *Classical Music: The 50 Greatest Composers and Their 1,000 Greatest Works* (New York: Ballantine Books, 1992), pp. 145–146.

3. The Holocaust Project—Selected Biographies—R (Rienzi, Cola di) (http://www.humanitas-international.org/holocaust/bios_r.htm).

4. William Shirer, *The Rise and Fall of the Third Reich* (New York: Simon and Schuster, 1960), p. 133.

5. Ibid., p. 135.

6. "Israeli Orchestra to Play Music by Wagner," *Truth News,* April 11, 2000 (http://truthnews.net/culture/2000_04_israel_wagner.html).

For Further Reading

For Young Adults

Cencetti, Greta. *Wagner.* New York: Peter Bedrick Books, 2001.

Getzinger, Donna, and Daniel Felsenfeld. *Richard Wagner and German Opera.* Greensboro, N.C.: Morgan Reynolds, 2004.

Samachson, Dorothy, and Joseph Samachson. *Masters of Music: Their Works, Their Lives, Their Times.* New York: Doubleday and Company, 1967.

Siberell, Anne. *Bravo! Brava! A Night at the Opera: Behind the Scenes with Composer, Cast and Crew.* New York: Oxford University Children's Books, 2001.

Works Consulted

Berger, William. *Wagner Without Fear.* New York: Vintage Books, 1998.

Deathridge, John, and Carl Dahlhaus. *The New Grove Wagner.* New York: W.W. Norton & Co., 1984.

Goulding, Phil G. *Classical Music: The 50 Greatest Composers and Their 1,000 Greatest Works.* New York: Ballantine Books, 1992.

Gutman, Robert W. *Richard Wagner: The Man, His Mind, and His Music.* New York: Time Life Records, 1972.

Millington, Barry. *Wagner.* New York: Vintage Books, 1987.

Panofsky, Walter. *Wagner: A Pictorial Biography.* New York: The Viking Press, 1963.

Schonberg, Harold. *The Lives of the Great Composers.* New York: W.W. Norton, 1981.

Shirer, William. *The Rise and Fall of the Third Reich.* New York: Simon and Schuster, 1960.

Watson, Derek. *Richard Wagner: A Biography.* New York: Schirmer Books, 1979.

On the Internet

The Classical Music Archives
http://www.classicalarchives.com/bios/codm/wagner.html

"Richard Wagner Biography"
http://www.pianoparadise.com/wagner.html

"Israeli Orchestra to Play Music by Wagner," *Truth News,* April 11, 2000
http://truthnews.net/culture/2000_04_israel_wagner.html

The Holocaust Project—Selected Biographies—R (Rienzi, Cola di)
http://www.humanitas-international.org/holocaust/bios_r.htm

About Hans Christian Andersen
http://www.underthesun.cc/Classics/Andersen/

Hans Christian Andersen (1805–1875)
http://www.kirjasto.sci.fi/hcanders.htm

Heinrich Schleimann
http://ragz-international.com/heinrich_schliemann.htm

Heinrich Schliemann, 1822–1890
http://www.mnsu.edu/emuseum/information/biography/pqrst/schliemann_heinrich.html

Orient Express
"The Truth Behind the Legend—The Orient Express"
http://www.seat61.com/Orient%20Express.htm

"American Orient Express"
http://www.railsnw.com/Tours/aoe/aoe.htm

Historic Figures—David Livingstone, Sir Henry Morton Stanley
http://www.bbc.co.uk/history/historic_figures/livingstone_david.shtml
http://www.bbc.co.uk/history/historic_figures/stanley_sir_henry_morton.shtml

David Livingstone National Memorial
http://www.biggar-net.co.uk/livingstone/

Smithsonian Magazine—"Stanley Meets Livingstone," October 2003
http://www.smithsonianmag.si.edu/smithsonian/issues03/oct03/livingstone.html

King Ludwig II
"The Swan King and His Castles"
http://www.german-way.com/german/ludwig.html

Neuschwanstein Castle—"King Ludwig II"—Short Biography
http://www.neuschwanstein.com/english/castle/ludwig/

Index